To your career success

Kate Prior

"Genius is one percent inspiration,
ninety-nine percent perspiration."
Thomas A. Edison

RESUME SUCCESS SECRETS

HOW TO WRITE A RESUME THAT GETS THE JOB!

Copyright © 2015 www.f2frecruitment.com.au

KATE PRIOR

#1 AMAZON BEST SELLING AUTHOR

Winner 2010 National Award for Small Business Champion – Recruitment Services

Finalist 2012 National Award for Small Business Champion – Recruitment Services

Managing Director, face2face Recruitment

www.f2frecruitment.com.au

QUANTITY PRINT ON DEMAND ORDERS

All titles by International Best Selling Author Kate Prior are available at special quantity discounts for bulk purchases to be included for marketing, promotions, fundraisers and/or educational purposes.

Free chapters are also available to promote to your clients or as a gift give away, with the option to purchase the full print or digital copy of the book.

To discuss how Kate can help accommodate your needs, simply contact kate@f2frecruitment.com.au or visit:

www.f2frecruitment.com.au

Suite 2, 16 Bentham Street, Yarralumla, ACT 2600

FREE TOOLS

Included in this book are these free gifts:

Job Tracker Form

http://www.f2frecruitment.com.au/resources/application-tracker/

Resume templates

http://www.f2frecruitment.com.au/resources/download-a-resume-template/

Reference check templates

http://www.f2frecruitment.com.au/latest-news/download-a-reference-check-template/

National Library of Australia

Cataloguing in Publication Entry

1st edition

ISBN: 978-0-9944771-1-8 (paperback)

DEDICATION

To Mum and Dad:

Thank you for never putting limitations on who you thought I could be or what I could do, and for believing in me.

I wish you were still here to see what you taught me put into practice.

"It is never too late to be what you might have been."
George Eliot

"Success is buried on the other side of frustration."
Tony Robbins

___

CONTENTS

INTRODUCTION..11

CHAPTER ONE: RESUMES.......................................15

CHAPTER TWO: HOW TO WORK WITH
RECRUITERS...45

CHAPTER THREE: REFEREES..............................59

CHAPTER FOUR: RESPONDING TO
GOVERNMENT POSITIONS......................................63

CHAPTER FIVE: RESPONDING TO POSITIONS ON
SEEK OR OTHER JOB BOARDS...............................83

CHAPTER SIX: PROFESSIONAL DIGITAL
FOOTPRINT...87

CHAPTER SEVEN: TRACKING POSITIONS AND
STATUS..97

CHAPTER EIGHT: STATE OF MIND AND
COMBATING NERVES..101

BONUS CHAPTER NINE: INTERVIEW TIPS.......113

ABOUT THE AUTHOR..147

"Our chief want is someone who will inspire us to be what we know we could be."
Ralph Waldo Emerson

INTRODUCTION

WHY THIS BOOK

The purpose of this book is to help you quickly and easily create a perfect resume that will go a long way towards getting your next job. Your resume is the only information a prospective employer has when deciding whether you should be selected for an interview. You need to get into an employer's head to know what they're thinking or seeking in a job candidate. Luckily for you, I have all the information you need in an easy-to-read and action format. This book provides you with free and valuable tools and resources, such as resume templates, a Job Tracker Form, videos, good and bad examples of how to present your resume to a prospective employer and how to present yourself at interview. All this information will enable you to create an effective resume to help secure that new position.

If you're out of work you're already facing enough pressure. You might be the sole bread winner or unexpectedly find yourself retrenched. You may be desperately trying to help your son or daughter find work before they become a long-term youth unemployment statistic.

This book is designed to cut to the chase. There are no fancy words. There is no long-winded information. Instead, this book provides you with what you need to take the first step toward finding work – an awesome resume.

The first part of this book leads you through how to create your spectacular resume, including examples. The second part covers preparation for and presentation at interview.

Hi there. I'm Kate Prior and I've been in recruitment for more than 20 years. Throughout my career I've worked with employers to help them understand what they're looking for in job seekers. I've also worked with job seekers to give them the highest possible chance of getting the job they desire.

During my career I've successfully placed more than 1,500 job seekers. In 2005 I started my own recruitment agency called face2face Recruitment. In 2010, my recruitment agency won a national award – Australian Small Business

Champion Award for Recruitment Services. In 2012, face2face Recruitment was a finalist in this same category.

Every time someone sits in front of me looking for a new job, I find myself providing the same advice over and over. My team does too. This was the catalyst for writing this book.

It's tough to be out there looking for work. I wanted to make it as easy as possible. Australia is experiencing its highest unemployment rates in decades. This means more people are looking for work and more people are competing for the position you want. It's so much easier when you have the tools you need to best present your resume and yourself.

I'm amazed that employers expect everyone to instinctively know how to write a great resume. Well that just isn't the case and why would it be? Writing a great resume is no different to anything else we do. We have to be taught and then we practice to refine our skills. No-one expects us to instinctively know the intricacies of painting a house, for example, including how to prepare a wall, tape windows, what type of paint to use, how many coats to apply and so on.

It's the same with creating a successful resume. We need guidance and training.

In this book I provide samples of resume templates you can quickly and easily use to create your job-getting resume. I've also included other tools for your arsenal to help you get the job. These have all been designed to provide you with tactics and the information you need. It's all designed to be as simple and fast as possible.

Remember that getting an interview from your resume is the first step in getting a job. The second step is performing well in the interview. Bonus Chapter 9, "Interview Tips", is designed specifically to help with this. It provides advice on combating your nerves, what type of questions to expect and ways to best answer them.

Ready? Let's get straight into it, starting with Chapter 1, "Resumes".

CHAPTER ONE

RESUMES

THE FIRST 60 SECONDS WILL SEAL YOUR FATE.

It can be confusing to understand what a successful resume should look like, especially with the unlimited supply of resume templates available. Which do you choose? Do you use a photo? How many pages should your resume be? What should you include in it? What's important and what isn't?

60 seconds. Yes, 60 seconds is how long a potential employer will spend scanning your resume to see if it goes into the "unsuitable" or "potential" pile.

The current job market is highly competitive with thousands looking for work. So it's no wonder that a potential employer generally only spends 60 seconds on an initial scan of each resume. If you don't outline your experience in a simple, clean format, you're at risk that highly relevant, important information on you and your skills will be overlooked.

Your goal as a job seeker is to stand out and show the employer why they should select you for interview. A great resume and excellent presentation at interview are the key elements of a successful job search.

Your prospective employer may have 40 to 70 resumes to go through. In today's world, everyone is being asked to do more in the same timeframe. So it's essential that your resume is scannable. That way your prospective employer can look at your resume and quickly ascertain that you have what they're looking for in the magic 60 seconds.

To make your resume scannable, you need white space, short, sharp bullet points and information tailored to the position. Pages full of text squashed together looks heavy, uninviting and too hard to read. You need to tailor your resume too. No longer can you get away with a generic resume that you simply send off with the hit of a button when responding to a job ad.

Here are two snapshots of resumes. The first is designed to be scanned in 60 seconds and the second is not. You'll see that the second resume is dense and presented in a difficult-to-read small font. You'll also see that it's trying to jam everything in. In doing so, it will lose the employer's attention and encourage them to quickly move to the next resume on the pile.

Which resume would you gravitate towards and scan if you were an employer? If you had 40 resumes sitting in front of you and limited time, would you even bother looking at the ones that are too hard to read? Or would you discard the resume while thinking: "This person has no idea how to present their resume."

Following are two examples of resumes, each with a different layout. Which would you choose to read?

SAMPLE 1: CLEAN, EASY TO READ

Organisation:	face2face Recruitment
Position:	Managing Director
Period:	February 2005 – Present

Kate started face2face Recruitment in February 2005 in Yarralumla, ACT. face2face Recruitment specialise in IT, HR, Administration Support, Sales and Finance. face2face supplies permanent and contract staff to government and the private sector.

Kate's duties and experience

- 15 years' experience in the recruitment industry

- 27 years' experience within government, recruitment and the IT industry in Canberra

- held positions such as Account Manager, Business Development Manager, Practice Manager and Managing Director

- proven background in managing two business arms simultaneously – ICT and HR,

- excellent experience in setting up a business in Canberra from scratch and expanding it into other states

- professional approach to her work, including an excellent standard of business ethics

- focused on providing an exceptional standard of work to clients

- expertise in rebuilding teams and maintaining high motivation levels among team members.

SAMPLE 2: POOR LAYOUT AND DENSE TEXT

face2face Recruitment – Managing Director – February 2005 – Present

Kate started face2face Recruitment in February 2005 in Yarralumla, ACT. Kate has had previous experience starting and growing companies for a number of recruitment firms. face2face Recruitment specialises in IT, HR, Administration Support, Sales and Finance. face2face supplies permanent and contract staff to government and the private sector. In a short time face2face has secured a number of preferred supplier arrangements with private sector clients and government.

face2face is also accredited with Government Endorsed Supplier Status and has already been supplying contractors to government agencies. Due to face2face's proven high level of service, the company is attracting great candidates across the board. This provides face2face and its clients with an advantage over its competition. Kate has 15 years' experience in the recruitment industry. Kate has 27 years' experience with government, recruitment, and the IT industry in Canberra. Kate has held positions such as Account Manager, Business Development Manager, Practice

Manager and Managing Director. Proven background managing two business arms simultaneously. At Company A, Kate managed the Professional Services Division and the IT Recruitment Division, while at Company B, she managed the IT and HR/Administration Support Recruitment arms. Excellent experience setting up a business in Canberra from scratch and expanding into other states. Kate has a professional approach to her work, which includes an excellent standard of business ethics. Kate is focused on providing an exceptional standard of service to clients, candidates and colleagues. Kate has an outstanding background in rebuilding teams and maintaining high motivation levels while encompassing a team focus. Kate has experience in developing business plans and budgets for a number of businesses. Kate has an ability to manage and develop staff to their full potential while keeping them motivated. Kate is well respected and known within the IT community in Canberra.

SIX KEY ELEMENTS OF A RESUME

A great resume requires six key elements. These are described here. To keep things as easy as possible I've included two resume templates you can choose from. These will lead you through the six key elements. The templates have been designed with your potential new employer in mind. They cover what employers look for and what they want to know. The template links are found later in this chapter.

Six key elements of a great resume

1. Front cover and contact details. This should include your name, email address, mobile or alternative contact number. It should include your citizenship (whether you're an Australian citizen or permanent resident or the type of visa you hold). It should also include when you're available to start work. You should list a Government Security Clearance or current and valid Police Check if you have them. I've described what these are in the next two paragraphs.

Government Security Clearance. Those who work for government are in most cases required to obtain a security clearance. This allows them to work with sensitive information. You can only gain a Government Security Clearance if you're employed by a government department and that department sponsors your application for a clearance. There's no other way to gain a Government Security Clearance.

Police Check. More and more employers are requesting that staff complete a Police Check. This is done by the Australian Federal Police. It provides a list of offences (if any) committed up to the time the form is submitted. Positions requiring you to work with vulnerable people and children always require a current Police Check. If you're working with money you'll usually have to have a current one, as your employer will want to know that you've never committed fraud. The cost of a Police Check is approximately $42. If you're able to, we suggest completing a Police Check and including it in your applications for work. It just gives the employer one less thing to think about before hiring you. If there are no offences this will also help build your credibility. This link takes you to the Police Check form:

http://www.afp.gov.au/what-we-do/police-checks/national-police-checks.aspx

Photo. Do you include or don't you? This is such a debated question. As a recruiter, whenever I see a well-groomed, well-presented person in a photo with a smile, I automatically want to read their resume. There are rules around including a photo, however. The photo should represent you as if you were on your way to an interview. Dress in professional attire. No 'happy snaps'. No photos of the fish you've caught with the boys (even though it's a huge fish). No photos of you in evening attire (even though you look absolutely amazing) and no photos in casual sports clothes. Instead, the photo you use should be shot anywhere from the waist up and include your chest, shoulders and your fabulous smiling face. You should also have great posture, don't slump. People with good posture look more alert; people who slump can be perceived as being lazy. I've included samples of great photos and bad photos further along.

Another reason I'm a fan of photos on resumes is that most employers will check if you have an online footprint (I cover this later in more detail). If you have an online footprint, an employer will see a photo of you on social media and it probably won't be as professional as the one on your resume. So providing a professional-looking photo provides balance. If by chance you don't use social media and other applicants do, then employers will see the photos of those competing for the job you want and, if they're good, this could disadvantage you.

Your resume photo doesn't have to be of you standing and looking uncomfortable, stiff and not yourself. By all means, display a little of your personality but don't go over the top. If you can, I strongly recommend getting a professional portrait photographer to take your photo. If this isn't an option, ask someone you know who is good with a camera to take the shot. The world isn't quite ready for selfies on resumes.

If you're getting someone you know to take your resume photo, help them get it right by showing them the sample photos in this book so they can replicate the style.

For decades many studies have shown that society treats attractive people more favourably. It's internally wired within us. Is it fair? Of course not. However, information is knowledge. So use this to your advantage, even if you're not one of the blessed beautiful people on earth. A well-groomed appearance, suitable professional clothing, a stylish haircut and a smile will go a long way to helping you get the interview, which is the second step to getting a job. Whether you like it or not, appearance counts, so do what you can to enhance yours. Yes fellas, I mean you too.

Your potential employer will place value on seeing a photo of a well-groomed, smartly presented person. A good photo may be enough to put you in front of some other candidates.

Here are photos showing great examples and bad examples of the same people to give you a perspective on the difference a fabulous resume photo can make. Not only that, you can see how you should present yourself for interview.

Great examples   **Bad examples**

Mature aged workers. If you're what society classes a "mature aged worker" you may feel you've been overlooked due to ageism. To combat this, it's advantageous for you to present yourself in a modern way, with sharp attire and a sharp haircut. If you wear glasses they should also be up with the current trends. This will go a long way to show that you're still switched on and "with it". I'm not agreeing that you should *have to do this*, but am providing you with knowledge that may help you.

Smile. The man in both of these photos is presented professionally and well groomed. But what a difference a SMILE makes! Who would you want to interview?

Entry level. When you're starting out you may not have a lot of funds to buy new clothes. Keeping your outfit smart and simple will do the job. How you dress for a day at school or university isn't how you would turn up for an interview. Your photo should represent how you would dress and present at interview. If you don't have something suitable, borrow from friends, siblings or even your Mum or Dad. Soon you'll have cash to splash.

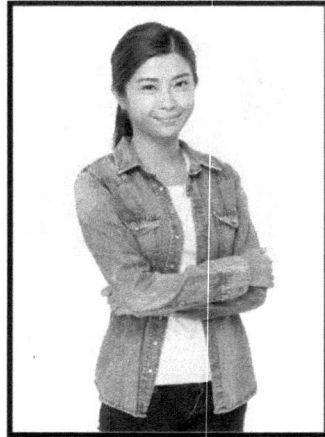

Blue collar and construction entry level. A suit for a labouring position may be over the top. For males, a nice polo shirt or smart shirt and trousers will do the trick. For females, a smart top and pant or skirt or simple dress would be appropriate. Just make sure you're well-groomed and that your clothes are wrinkle free. Never use a holiday snap as a photo on your resume.

White collar and professional roles – suit up. What a difference a suit makes. It's always better to overdress for an interview than under dress. The expectation is that you should be at your best for an interview. The same goes for the photo you choose for your resume.

Are you serious? Show your prospective employer that you're serious about your interview and job opportunity. Even though the photo on the right has the man well-groomed and trendy, you wouldn't use this as a resume photo. The photo on the left says you're ready for the job interview.

Eye contact. You should be looking straight ahead in your photo because it provides better eye contact and is more engaging than a photo taken in profile.

2. Overview. In your resume's overview, include 10 to 12 bullet points outlining your strengths for the role. Include soft skills. This is covered in more detail later. Match the bullet points against the job description and/or task list provided for the position you're applying for. You should tailor this for every position you apply for. You should also use the same language listed in the job description. This will make it easier for the employer to see you're a match for what they want. It's also useful to **highlight/bold** some key words or phrases to make them stand out and help the employer scan. Don't go overboard, however. Each bullet point should only have a couple of words or one short phrase **highlighted/bolded**. Don't be complacent or lazy. In your overview you should use strong, power words, like "**extensive** experience", rather than just "experience". Try "has **expertise**" rather than "has a background in".

Once you've completed your overview, check that you've mirrored and/or used the same descriptions for tasks as the employer and make sure you change them throughout the body of your resume as well. For example, if the ad for the position uses "Retail Officer", then you should use that term as well, rather than say, "Shop Assistant". Mirroring the same language helps increase your chances of being selected for interview as the employer is familiar with the wording and will be scanning for it.

3. Education and courses. List your degrees, academic qualifications and relevant courses you've completed. List these in reverse chronological order (the most recent first). Include the name of the organisation that conducted the training, the name of the degree or course you completed and the year you completed it. If you're a mature aged worker, you may choose to leave off the year you completed your degree or diploma.

4. Experience in reverse chronological order. This includes organisations you've worked with, a short paragraph about what each does, the start and finish date of each position, your job title, your duties and tasks and one or two major achievements for each position.

5. Hobbies and interests. Listing your hobbies and interests enables your potential employer to get a better understanding of who you are. If selected for interview, the employer may use this type of information as an ice breaker to get the conversation going and give you time to relax into the interview. The potential employer may also have some of the same interests as you, which usually works in your favour because it can lead to a relaxed, two-way conversation at the start of the interview. Your hobbies or interests might include cooking, travel, reading, playing chess, bush walking, playing sports or volunteering with not-for-profits.

6. Referees. You have three options for listing referees. The first is to state "Referees provided on request". The second is to list two suitable referees with their contact details who have agreed in advance to act as your referee. The third is to supply one written reference with your application and state "Additional referees provided on request". Referees are a very important part of the job-seeking process. This is covered in more detail later.

Want to jump in and get started using one of the resume templates? You'll find them through the link below. However, to get the most from this book and to give yourself the best chance of landing that position you so badly want or need, I strongly suggest reading the remaining chapters.

Link to resume templates

http://www.f2frecruitment.com.au/resources/download-a-resume-template/

Optional video introduction. You also have the option of producing a short video in which you tell your prospective employer a bit about yourself. You can include this as a link in your resume if you're sending it by email or online.

Not everyone finds it easy to sit in front of a camera and talk about themselves. My research reveals that if there's an option for an employer to look at a short video introduction of a candidate they'll do so before reading a resume. If the candidate presents well in the video they're usually selected for interview. This can be a huge differentiator.

Your video should be 40 to 60 seconds long. You can use your phone or a video camera. If you're not able to incorporate a link to your video in your resume, then the next best thing is to put it onto a USB port and deliver it in person. If you do this, please make sure you're dressed professionally and well-groomed.

Get some friends to tell you what they think of your video. For example, do you look comfortable and relaxed? If you have mixed or bad reviews from your trusted critics, then leave the video out.

The easiest way to place your video into your resume is through a Dropbox account (www.dropbox.com). Dropbox is a free cloud storage solution that you can access through a computer, smartphone and tablet. Within your Dropbox account you'll find a "public folder" that enables you to provide a link so anybody can open that file. No password is required.

Upload your finished video to the public folder. Once you've done so, click 'share' and you can copy the Public link to the file to insert the video into your resume. This link can be added by highlighting the text you wish to link. Then right click and select Open Hyperlink. Add the copied link to the address bar, and your video will now open and play automatically when you click on the linked text. See this example:

http://www.f2frecruitment.com.au/videos/rssvideos/

RESUME STYLING – KEEP IT CONSISTENT

Your resume should be easy to read and understand. This includes using plain, consistent and professional language.

Always use bullet points when outlining your duties in positions. Each bullet point should be no more than 1.5 lines in length. If longer, the bullet point becomes a small paragraph and the information is no longer scannable. Remember, most employers will only spend **60 seconds** scanning your resume.

Bullet points are much easier to read and they ensure that important information doesn't get lost. Each bullet point should only cover one topic. They're very powerful.

Make sure you use the same style, format, font and size throughout your resume. Following a strict format will keep your resume looking professional. You should use standard fonts such as Arial or Calibri and 11 or 12 point size.

Never use 8 or 10 point font for your resume. This size is harder to read than an 11 or 12 point font. It's better to have a resume that's a little longer than it is to use an 8 point font to shorten the number of pages. People can choose if they want to read the last couple of pages. Choosing a tiny font that's hard to read makes scanning difficult. All your efforts may be in vain and your resume will inevitably land on the "too hard to read" pile, which is ultimately the "unsuitable pile".

Your resume should be no more than five pages. Anything longer is too long. You might find this challenging because you want to get everything in that you've done. Remember, however, that employers are most interested in what your last two to three positions were, not what you did 10 or 15 years ago.

WHAT YOU SHOULD INCLUDE

If your resume is well over five pages you need to cut it down. Focus on your last two to three roles and list the tasks you performed under each one. For previous positions simply list the job title, length of time in the position and the organisation you worked for. Leave the duties out with these previous positions. This will enable the employer to scan through your resume, see your history, understand your background and determine how you progressed to where you are today. Notice on the last position in the next example how not every role is listed. Doing so would be going too far back. This is what recruiters call truncating a resume. Instead, this example simply states there were various roles before 1997.

Mature aged workers. The tips I've outlined earlier for what to include in a resume are also useful for mature aged workers. Not going too far back is also a strategic tactic because it doesn't make your age obvious which means your age can't be used as a negative.

Example

Position:	Manager
Timeframe:	July 2005 – December 2011
Organisation:	face2face Recruitment Pty Ltd

Position:	Manager
Timeframe:	January 2000 – June 2005
Organisation:	Consulting Services Australia

Position:	Team Leader
Timeframe:	July 1997 – December 1999
Organisation:	Resources Company Pty Ltd

Position:	Various sales, recruitment and administrative roles
Timeframe:	Prior to July 1997
Organisation:	Various organisations, available if required

Graduates and school leavers. If you're a recent graduate or are at the early stages of your career, include any work experience completed, any major projects completed while studying and any volunteer experience. Have a look at advertisements for the roles you might be interested in and make sure you capture relevant experience and skills. This should include paid work, volunteering, or what you've achieved as part of a university project or work experience.

It's also important for you to cover your personality traits. Talk about the things you believe you're good at. It could be the time management skills you developed while juggling studying and working part-time job at a major supermarket. You may have great attention to detail or excel at dealing with people. You might be reliable and enthusiastic. You might have strong Microsoft Office skills or the skill to learn quickly.

WHAT NOT TO DO

Don't include a "Career objective" at the beginning of your resume. Job seekers are sometimes overlooked because what they've listed as their career objective doesn't match that of the potential employer. This information can also easily be misinterpreted. For example, you may say you want to be the manager of the company you're applying to work for. You may mean eventually – down the track – but if you only have 12 months' experience your potential employer may think that you're impatient and simply don't understand how far off you are from being management material. They may assume that they'll therefore have trouble managing your expectations and go to the next person in the pile.

Another example is when a "Career Objective" states that you want to become a research analyst even though you've just left school or university and are applying for a basic administration role. The potential employer may in this case think that you're only applying for this role because it's the only one available right now. The employer may conclude that you'll leave as soon as something better comes up.

Treat your resume seriously and take some time writing it. If you're not 100 percent happy with it, take some time away from it and return later with fresh eyes. Your resume is your first and last chance at gaining an interview for the role you're applying for. Don't rush it. This is such an important document you need to take time to develop it and look at it several times. Each time you do so, you'll probably think of some great additional skills that you'd forgotten about or previously didn't think were relevant.

Never send your resume out without having run the computer's Australian/English spell checker over it (never an American spell checker). Make sure you don't make spelling mistakes as each one will be noticed and this may signal your lack of attention to detail. Spell checker will also help with grammar and provide other suggestions for improving your wording. Many employers won't tolerate spelling mistakes in a resume and will discard it. Some people really have a "bee in their bonnet" when it comes to errors in resumes. They're concerned that if you can't get it right in a document as important as your resume, you might not get it right with important documents you'd be sending out on their behalf.

Never send out your resume without at least one other person proofreading it. Ideally you want at least two people to read your resume. One might be good at identifying grammar issues or where phrasing could be improved. The other might be great at fixing spelling errors and at picking up words spelled correctly but in the wrong context, such as "there" and "their" or "hear" and "here".

Don't include personal information such as your age, religion, marital status or how many children you have. This information could be used to discriminate against you. So, rather than looking at the experience in your resume, someone may make a decision that you're too young or too old for the position.

TIPS TO MAKE YOUR RESUME STAND OUT

For each role you've performed, write a short paragraph about what the organisation you worked for does. The paragraph should be three to four lines long. This will then put your skills and tasks into perspective for the potential employer.

At the end of each position, include one or two achievements you've accomplished in the position.

Overview

By including a 10 to 12 bullet point overview on the cover page of your resume you will show the employer your strengths against the job description. This is also where you should highlight your "soft skills" that suit this position. Soft skills are personality traits that cannot be demonstrated by your experience or skills. Examples of soft skills are being proactive, having a strong work ethic, being a problem solver, being adaptable, being a collaborative person and a team player, having great communication skills, having time management skills, having the ability to accept and learn from constructive criticism, being self-confident and/or having the ability to work well under pressure.

It's crucial to tailor the overview on the cover page for each position you're applying for. Every position will have a different flavour so read the job description and tasks carefully. Highlight the most important requirements for the position. Then make sure your overview includes bullet points that capture these. This will enable the employer to quickly scan your cover page and pick up on your strengths for the position. This will encourage them to continue reading your resume. You need to, however, ensure that these bullet points are also included in your main resume, to increase your chances of getting an interview.

Tailoring your resume for a particular role

Take the extra time to add information about your skills and experiences that are relevant to the job requirements. Read the job description and tick off all the tasks you have experience in. Make sure you include the tasks in the body of your resume under the position for which you completed them. If you completed the same tasks in several positions, make sure you list them under each position you held. Never put "same as above". To make them look different, change the order and wording slightly. If you think hard enough about it, you'll usually find you've completed some tasks that are unique to each position.

Extra activities and hobbies

When you list your hobbies or interests, a potential employer may use these as an ice breaker when interviewing you. An ice breaker is a question asked or comment made to start a conversation. You'll never know what people you might meet and what interests they might have. If the employer has similar hobbies to you, this can help get the conversation started in a more relaxed and less stressful manner. This is always a better option for you when being interviewed. It gives you time to settle into the interview and get rid of some nerves.

This information also helps the employer get a better understanding of who you are. It enables them to start compiling an idea of whether you'll suit the organisation's environment.

CHAPTER TWO

HOW TO WORK WITH RECRUITERS

BENEFITS OF WORKING WITH A RECRUITER

Did you know there's no cost to you to use the services of a recruiter? The organisation who employs you pays the recruiter so the service you get is FREE.

As with any industry there are always organisations that stand out from the others. It's the same with recruitment companies. One thing you'll want to look out for is a recruiter who provides you with excellent service. These days this means a recruiter who will provide you with a personalised service by offering to help you with your resume and prepare you for interview with an employer. If you can find a recruiter who is willing to treat you like a client, then stick with them.

It's worthwhile completing some online searches to find the recruiter who best suits you. If you're looking for a construction role, for example, you'll be able to find a recruiter who specialises in construction through an Internet search. Just make sure the recruiters you select have roles you want to apply for. If a recruiter, for example, specialises in hospitality and you want an administrative position, you won't want to register with that recruiter.

Did you know that a large percentage of positions available only go to recruiters? Organisations normally don't have the time or expertise to recruit, so they outsource their recruitment requirements to a recruitment agency. Therefore, if you're not registered with a number of agencies in your area, you're missing out on opportunities to find a new job.

I've looked but haven't been able to find statistics on how many positions go through recruitment agencies. Based on my direct experience, I would suggest it would be in the vicinity of 40 percent.

Some of the many benefits of working with a great recruiter

- provide job seekers with a FREE service

- have jobs on their books that are exclusive to them, which means less competition for roles

- they search their database of registered job seekers suitable for the position and hopefully find you

- help you with your resume, provide advice and a suitable resume template

- help prepare you for interview if you're shortlisted

- provide a lot more information and background about the company seeking a new employee than what's usually advertised

- understand the culture of the company and if you're a suitable match

- fast track the recruitment process for you

- are able to submit resumes for government non-ongoing or temporary roles which, in the vast majority of cases, don't require you to complete a selection criteria

- are experts at presenting you in the best possible light to the employer (at least the good ones do)

- always have your best interest at heart and be able to tell you the positives about a potential position and if there are issues to be aware of.

HOW TO SELECT THE RIGHT RECRUITMENT AGENCY

As with any industry, all companies are not the same. You want to develop a working relationship with those that stand out from the rest. You want a recruiter who will help you develop your resume, have templates you can use, be available to talk to on the phone and meet in person.

Your recruiter should always want to do the best thing by you and genuinely care about finding you a role. They'll provide advice on what's happening in the job market and what's trending. They'll listen to what you're seeking for your next role. You may, for example, want to change direction with your career or step back a bit and not work in such high-pressure roles. You may be a return-to-work mum or dad or may need extra money in semi-retirement to make ends meet. No matter what your circumstances, a good recruiter will develop a plan of attack to get you the outcome you want.

Use the Internet to research recruiters who operate in the geographic area and/or city you want to work in and who cover the types of positions you're interested in.

Recruitment consultants are the eyes of the potential employer. Getting in front of one can be much harder than you may think. Today, I would imagine most recruitment companies receive between 200 and 400 new job seekers a month. Recruiters are generally very hard working and have a great deal of pressure placed on them every day. They're pulled in all directions and work well above a 40-hour week. But they'll notice *you* if you follow the steps I outline next.

HOW TO STAND OUT TO A RECRUITER

You need to provide the recruiter with a quick synopsis of who you are, what you're looking for and all other information they need. If you've given them all of this and have attached a great resume, you're doing better than 85 percent of the others registering with the recruiter. The easier it is for the recruiter to work with you, the better your chance of gaining employment.

The first step is to create a solid resume that captures your skills and talents. To help, use one of the templates provided in Chapter 1. You might be thinking: "Isn't the recruiter supposed to help me with a resume?" I would love to say "yes", but it may not always be the case and I don't want you to miss out on roles they may have.

People who take initiative and control of a situation always do better than those who sit back and wait for someone to drag them along. Remember, there's a lot of competition out there with some of the highest unemployment figures Australia has seen in decades. If you want a role with that fantastic company, then you're going to have to fight for it.

The second step is to create a great introduction email to send with your resume. When dealing directly with a recruiter it's better to put all relevant information into an email rather than attaching a separate cover letter. Many employers and recruiters won't read a cover letter because they simply don't have the time. Any important information should therefore be in your resume. The value of including an introductory email to a recruiter is provided later in this chapter.

Another reason not to attach a separate cover letter relates to the way recruitment software works. Most good recruitment software automatically captures your resume on the file created, as well as all emails sent between you and your recruiter. It doesn't, however, capture your cover letter.

Your introduction email to your recruiter should state

- The type of work you're looking for. Is it Office Manager, Finance Manager, Data Entry, Reception, Account Manager, Labourer, Scientist, Retail Assistant, Manager, Technician? If you're open to a number of roles let the recruiter know. You can also let them know what you're definitely *not* interested in. The more information the recruiter has, the better they can serve you.

- When you're available to start work. Is it a specific day and month or do you need two weeks' notice or four weeks' notice? Are you available immediately?

- Your citizenship and, where necessary, visa status. Are you an Australian citizen or permanent resident? Are you able to work on a student or work visa? There's no point in starting a process only to discover that the employer can't accept you because you're in Australia on a visa.

- Your preference for the type of work you want. Is it temporary or contract work? Permanent full-time or permanent part-time? Let the recruiter know if you'll consider temporary work while waiting for the right permanent role. It's surprising how many people start with an organisation on a temporary basis and are then taken on as permanent employee because they've done a great job.

- Your range of salary expectation. Is it, for example, $50,000 to $55,000 plus superannuation? For temporary work list the hourly rate. Is it, for example, $30 plus superannuation? By stating *plus superannuation* you'll avoid confusion around salary. Some companies refer to a remuneration package that includes the superannuation component and base salary, while others only discuss the base salary. Government organisations only discuss salary in terms of base salary. It's therefore important when talking to a recruiter to be clear about your salary. The best way is to state it this way: "I want $xx plus superannuation."

- Whether you have a current Police Check, current Government Security Clearance or relevant certification required for the positions you're interested in (such as a Cert IV in Business Administration). More and more organisations are seeking to employ people who already have a current Police Check. This shows if you have a criminal history. People working in finance roles usually have to complete a Police Check. A Police Check costs around $42. If you have a clean slate, it's just one more thing in your favour that someone else may not have.

- A little bit about yourself, including the softs skills covered in Chapter 1. Don't forget to also list these soft skills in the overview of your resume.

You should also attach with your introduction email a professional photograph of yourself. Remember to also include this photograph in your resume if you have decided to use one. I would recommend that you do, as long as you've followed the rules about photographs listed in Chapter 1.

I've provided a sample email on the next page.

Hello Charlie:

I would like to register with XYZ Recruitment as I have noticed in the past you have had roles that would suit my capabilities and skill set. Please find my resume attached. It would be great if I could meet you in person, since I know that makes such a difference.

So that you understand what I am looking for and to streamline the process, I have set out below the information I think you would require. To help you remember me I have attached my photo.

Information and details:
Kate Prior
0403 659 812
02 6344 6500
kate@pleasefindmeajob.com.au – preferred contact method or SMS

- available to start with two days' notice
- Australian citizen and living in ACT

- have a current Police Check, valid for another four months
- preference is for a permanent position, but will take temp work while looking
- my perfect role would be a CEO, but will also look at General Manager and Manager roles
- for a CEO role I'm ideally after a salary of $100,000 to $120,000 plus superannuation (or $60 to $70 an hour)
- my qualification: Cert IV in Business and Administration

Snapshot of myself:

- more than 20 years as a CEO and Senior Manager
- worked in ICT, training and recruitment
- focused and outcomes driven
- have a collaborative approach to managing teams
- have exceptional organisational skills
- am excellent in stakeholder engagement, liaison and negotiation skills
- am enthusiastic
- am visionary.

Please call and/or email any roles you think may be suitable.

Regards
(add signature block)

Optional, but so worth it. If you're up to it and can present relaxed in front of a camera, I recommend a video introduction. The recruiter will snap you up. A sample of a video introduction is available through the link below. Simply take the video on your phone and send it to the recruiter's mobile, or incorporate it as link in your resume or your introduction email. Again this will make you stand out from hundreds of people registering. The recruiter will automatically see how you present and get a glimpse of your personality.

VIDEOS CAN BE LINKED DIRECTLY INTO YOUR EMAIL, BY USING A FREE DROPBOX ACCOUNT.

See sample video:

http://www.f2frecruitment.com.au/videos/rssvideos/

Don't be a stalker. When dealing with a recruitment agency it's important not to stalk them with constant emails and phone calls. This will do nothing to help your cause. In fact, it may make the recruiter change their mind about you. If you want to follow up, I suggest that contacting the recruiter once a week is acceptable. If the recruiter says they should know something in two weeks, then wait until after the two weeks to follow up if you haven't heard.

If you're registered with a recruiter and aren't hearing from them regularly, touch base every three weeks. This will put you top of mind for any roles that come in.

CHAPTER THREE

REFEREES

PREPARING YOUR REFEREES

When asking people to be your referee, you want to be confident they'll provide a fair and favourable assessment of your work and soft skills. If you don't think this will be the case, then find another referee. Employers and recruiters ideally want two relatively recent referees. They should understand that it's very difficult to provide a referee from your current workplace if they don't know you're looking for a new role. Your confidentiality needs to be protected.

You should also confirm with the referee that they'll have time to take and potentially respond to several phone calls seeking their input. Many organisations have an internal process stating that two verbal reference checks must be completed before an applicant can be offered the role. If your referee doesn't make themselves available, it could damage your chance of getting the position.

If you haven't worked for a while and have a hard copy (printed) reference from your last employer that will usually count as one. Your new employer or recruiter will also want to speak to a referee on the phone. Be prepared and have their contact details available.

If you can't get a reference from your last manager, see if you can find a client or a former colleague who will vouch for you. Character (from a personal friend) referees are not usually accepted.

Where possible, see if your best referee will complete a reference check and email it to you (see sample below). This way you can send it in with your application. This is powerful and will give you instant credibility. Again, this will add strength to your application since it will take away some of the questions prospective employers will have. It may also save your referee from being constantly contacted every time you're short-listed for a position. It will be considered valid since the employers will be able to see the contact details for the reference included in the reference check. The following link includes two basic reference check templates. One is for a manager who would have staff reporting to them and the other is for an employee without management responsibility.

REFERENCE CHECK

Referee check for:

Date:

Name of referee:

Position of referee:

Company represented:

Contact phone:

Contact email:

Questions:

- Were you Xxxx's direct supervisor? For how long? If no, what was your working relationship with Xxxx?

- How would you describe Xxxx's reliability with punctuality and attendance?

---

http://www.f2frecruitment.com.au/latest-news/download-a-reference-check-template/

To help your referees give you the best report, provide them with a copy of the job description. This way they can put questions they're asked into perspective. If they feel you did a great job for them and respect you, they'll go the extra mile and add additional positive information relevant to the job description you've provided.

CHAPTER FOUR

RESPONDING TO GOVERNMENT POSITIONS

DEMYSTIFYING GOVERNMENT LINGO

Lingo	Meaning/description
APS	Australian Public Service
ASP1, APS2, APS3, APS4, APS5, APS6	Australian Public Service Level 1, 2, 3 etc. These are designated levels, with 1 being entry level. The higher the level the more responsibility. Levels 5 and 6 may include overseeing the work of others.
EL1 and EL2	Executive Level 1 and Executive Level 2. These are usually management roles that require leadership and mentoring. Usually by the time people are in these

	positions they may have a speciality in a particular area.
SES	Senior Executive Band 1, 2 or 3. These are also referred to as Assistant Secretary or Secretary of a department. These are the most senior roles in a department. The Secretary of a department usually reports directly to the Minister of that department.
Ongoing	This is what the private sector calls a permanent position.
Non-ongoing	Non-ongoing employees fill short to medium-term vacancies. Usually the assignment can't be extended beyond 12 months. This type of position is usually for filling a role while someone is on extended leave, maternity leave or while an ongoing recruitment process is taking place. The department pays you as if you're a permanent employee. While

	working you accumulate annual leave and sick leave. You're also paid for public holidays.
Temp/Contract	This is where you're engaged, usually on shorter term assignments from a few days to a couple of months. You'll be paid only for actual hours worked. There are no entitlements to accrue annual or sick leave.
Incumbent	This is another term for someone who is acting in a position. This means the person is in the position until the employer can find a permanent or ongoing person to fill the position.
Merit-based	In 2008, the Australian Government introduced a policy implementing transparent and merit-based assessment for selecting most Australian Public Service positions. In essence this was designed so no-one would have an

	advantage or be disadvantaged when applying for and being selected for government positions.

DIFFERENCES BETWEEN GOVERNMENT AND PRIVATE SECTOR

Residency status. When applying for Australian Government roles, applicants must be Australian citizens. Local governments will usually accept applicants with Permanent Residency status. In most cases people coming to Australia on a visa won't be eligible to work in the Australian Government, state or territory government or local government organisations.

In Chapter 1, I discussed private sector resumes and the key elements required to produce a successful one. These same principles apply when writing a resume for government.

The major difference is that a private sector resume has an overview of bullet points highlighting your strengths against the job description and tasks required. With a government position you're required to respond to selection criteria. The selection criteria takes most people between seven and 10 hours to complete. With government resumes you wouldn't normally supply a short video.

When applying for a government contract or non-ongoing role through a recruitment agency, you won't be required – in the vast majority of cases – to complete selection criteria. Instead, you'll usually only have to provide 10 to 12 bullet points highlighting your strengths.

Government selection criteria. The first time you complete selection criteria is always going to be the most difficult. Once you have that experience under your belt, it becomes a lot easier. In some cases you'll find the criteria will be very similar from one position to another.

Later is this chapter, under "Selection Criteria", I include some links that are useful for "breaking the code" when responding to government selection criteria.

With government positions the selection criteria plays a critical role. You'll be deemed suitable or unsuitable based purely on your response. Your resume will usually not be read at this stage. However it's still important to have a great resume as it will probably be referenced later when you're completing an interview.

Some recruitment companies will complete selection criteria on your behalf. The up side is that once you've completed one response and understand what's expected you can probably handle the next one yourself. The down side is that if you haven't been involved in the process of responding to the selection criteria and are selected for interview there's a big chance you may not perform well at interview. You'll be asked questions based on the selection criteria and if you don't have an understanding of what's written or if the responses have been exaggerated you'll struggle and even crash and burn in the interview.

If you use a professional selection criteria writer, you must read and understand the responses they've written on your behalf. Usually such a professional writer will follow the STAR (Situation/Task/Action/Result) method of responding. A good writer will involve you in the process. It's understandable why people use a selection criteria writer as many struggle to complete the criteria, which can take up to 10 hours. If you've not been employed by government before you may opt for this solution to cope with what's otherwise a daunting process. Under "Selection Criteria", I've included links explaining the STAR method of responding to selection criteria and interview questions.

You can find a professional selection criteria writer by completing an Internet search for "professional selection criteria writers". Prices vary greatly. The more personalised the service the more it will cost, but the better it will be for you. Usually this can cost between $250 and $400 depending on the level of position you're after and how strong your resume is. This is pretty good value when you consider it could take you up to two days and be frustrating. If you go down this path, do your research and find a good writer who wants to talk to you and involve you in the process.

Scribes. Government departments use scribes to help with recruitment rounds. Scribes can be hired to shortlist candidates purely on their response to selection criteria. They won't look at your resume so it's important to get the selection criteria right when applying for government roles.

Scribes are also hired to sit in on interviews with the interview panel and take notes to prepare a report on how individuals performed. The reports are then provided to the

Chair of the interview panel and are used to decide who will secure the role or roles available.

Suitable/unsuitable. When a scribe or government employee shortlist candidates, they rank them as "suitable" or "unsuitable" based purely on their response to the selection criteria. If you're deemed suitable you'll proceed to interview. If you've been deemed unsuitable you may not be notified of this until the recruitment process is completed.

Timelines. With private enterprise the recruitment process usually takes between four and six weeks from start to finish. With government, it usually takes between 12 and 16 weeks (in some cases longer).

Follow up. If you were selected for interview and the contact gives you a timeframe for when they'll have an outcome, only call after that timeframe. For example, if the contact indicates they'll come back to you in a week, then contact them only after that week has passed. Don't chase people every day or every second day. This won't hasten the process.

If you've submitted an application with the private sector, usually wait for two weeks after the job has closed to follow up. It's a good idea to turn on the "Request a delivery receipt" and "Request a read receipt" functions on your computer.

Microsoft Office will then send you an email when your email and resume have arrived with the contact, and another when your email has been read. When creating an email to send with your application, you'll find on top of your screen an "Options" menu pick. Click on "Options", then click the box for each receipt.

With government roles, the process can be a lot longer. Normally your contact will be able to provide timeframes for when they expect the process to be complete.

BEFORE APPLYING FOR GOVERNMENT ROLES, ASK YOUR CONTACT THESE TWO QUESTIONS

1. Is there an incumbent in the role?
2. If so, how long have they been acting in the position?

These two questions may save you a lot of time and energy completing a selection criteria. If an incumbent has been acting in the role for a relative short time, say one to two months, I would strongly suggest applying.

If an incumbent has been acting in the position for a longer time, say eight months or more, they'll have a strong understanding of the position and have developed a professional relationship and networks within the team. This doesn't mean they'll automatically get the role—they have to go through the process, just like you do. However, it would be no surprise that they would understand the position extremely well, be able to complete a powerful selection criteria and be able to perform well in interview.

There are no guarantees for an incumbent acting in a position, however. While they may be in the position and performing the duties very well, they might not be great during an interview. I haven't been able to source published statistics on the percentage of people acting in positions for more than six months who have or have not succeeded in securing the role. Purely based on my experience and talking to a large number of scribes, I would suggest that approximately 50 percent of incumbents will win the position.

So what's the upshot of all of this? Since completing a selection criteria can be arduous and stressful, why not focus on a role that's new, a role that doesn't have anyone acting in it, a role that's currently available or a role in which someone has only been acting for a short time? Your chances of success should be higher.

GOVERNMENT RECRUITMENT AND SELECTION PROCESS

The Australian Government follows a strict "Order of Merit System" when processing applications for a position. Detailed information on this is on the Australian Public Service Commission's website. The process is detailed and involves a lot of steps, forms and approvals before a position can even be advertised. For now, it's not essential to review this. I've provided this information in case you're interested in how the whole process works.

Later in this chapter you'll find links under "Selection Criteria" that provide a guide, examples and information on the process government uses.

GOVERNMENT SHORT-LISTING PROCESS

Government has a stringent process for short-listing applicants. To provide you with a better understanding of what this process is, you'll find, on the next page, a sample template of what the Scribe or Selection Panel needs to short-list applicants. Along with the sample table, an individual assessment report will be completed on your performance at interview.

Sample template for short-listing (APS Recruitment guidelines) is on the next page.

SHORT-LISTING MATRIX

Date	Position number
Branch/section	Position title

Selection criteria	
A	B
C	D
E	F

Applicant name	Score for each selection criteria						Overall assessment
	A	B	C	D	E	F	

Rating scale

This can be used for short-listing purposes as well as for individual and comparative assessments.

Scale	Description	Performance indicators
Highly suitable 8 –10	Candidate possesses exceptionally well-developed and relevant skills, abilities and personal qualities. They could be relied upon to perform consistently to a high standard.	Candidate has the ability to perform at a high level without direct supervision for one or more of these reasons: • excellent job knowledge • exceptionally reliable and responsible • considerable demonstrated ability in problem solving and change management.
Suitable 5–7	Candidate possesses well-developed and relevant skills, abilities and personal qualities. They could be relied upon to achieve	Candidate would require minimal direct supervision to achieve good results, for one or more of these reasons:

	good results with limited supervision.	• reliable and responsible • sound job knowledge • suggests and initiates improvements • deals with all routine and most complex matters.
Unsuitable 0 – 4	Candidate is unable to demonstrate the relevant skills, abilities and personal qualities required for the position.	Candidate would be unable to perform the duties to the standard required and would require some supervision for one or more of these reasons: • limited job knowledge • lacks some essential skills required to perform the role • work performance is inconsistent and makes errors

	• work output is poor • has difficulty dealing with routine matters and solving problems.

OVERALL ASSESSMENT

Overall assessment of the applicant	
Scale	**Description**
Highly suitable (HS)	Majority of the selection criteria assessed as highly suitable.
Suitable (S)	Majority of the selection criteria assessed as suitable.
Unsuitable (NS)	Majority of the selection criteria assessed as unsuitable.

SELECTION CRITERIA

With government positions you're responding to directly, you'll be required to complete a selection criteria. If you don't complete a selection criteria your application will be deemed non-compliant and you won't be considered.

Government suggests that you respond to the selection criteria using the STAR method.

S = **Situation** – Provide a brief outline of the situation or setting

T = **Task** – What was your role?

A = **Actions** – What did you do and how did you do it?

R = **Results** – Describe the outcomes. What did you achieve?

The Australian Government has excellent information that's easy to follow to help you when responding to selection criteria. This link provides all the information you need to know on how to respond to selection criteria.

http://www.jobaccess.gov.au/employees-jobseekers/getting-work/how-apply-job/how-write-selection-criteria

Below is another source of information and tips from the Australian Public Service Commission website. This link provides access to a fact sheet to help you respond to government selection criterion.

http://www.apsc.gov.au/publications-and-media/current-publications/cracking-the-code/factsheet5

The Australian Government's JobAccess website also has useful information and free assistance for those with a disability.

More information on this and the free resources available at: http://www.jobaccess.gov.au/disability-work

GOVERNMENT SECURITY CLEARANCE

What's a security clearance? A security clearance provides you with authorisation to access classified information that would otherwise not be accessible. Your suitability to hold a security clearance is determined by the type of information you'll be required to access to do your job.

To obtain a Government Security Clearance, you need to undergo a number of assessments and background checks. These are undertaken to make sure you're eligible, suitable and can be relied on to safeguard security classified information and/or resources.

Australian citizenship is a mandatory condition for eligibility to gain a security clearance.

The Australian Government Security Vetting Agency is responsible for processing and granting security clearances for the Australian, state and territory governments.

You can't instigate or pay to complete a clearance for yourself. Clearances have to be sponsored by the department or agency.

This table outlines the types of clearances, approximate cost to departments and approximate time it takes for a clearance to be provided once you've completed all required paper work.

Types of government security clearances

Old terminology	New terminology	Approximate cost
Protected/Restricted Confidential/Highly Protected	Baseline Vetting	$434.39

Secret	Negative Vetting 1 (NV1)	$1,118.04
Top Secret (Negative Vetting)	Negative Vetting 2 (NV2)	$2,092.09
Top Secret (Positive Vetting)	Positive Vetting (PV)	$9,226.25

Clearance level	Approximate time to process	Clearance longevity
Baseline Vetting	1 month	15 years
Negative Vetting 1 (NV1)	4 months	10 years
Negative Vetting 2 (NV2)	6 months	5 years
Positive Vetting (PV)	6 – 8 months	2.5 years

CHAPTER FIVE

RESPONDING TO POSITIONS ON SEEK OR OTHER JOB BOARDS

When creating your resume, follow the principles outlined in Chapter 1. When responding to a job board you can include a cover letter, however it may not be read or forwarded to the appropriate person.

If you decide to write a cover letter make sure it's concise and includes a synopsis of why you believe you're suitable for the position. Your cover letter should be less than a page long. The information you provide should be a combination of short paragraphs and bullet points. Information in long paragraphs will be lost to the reader. Remember that this letter will also be scanned. If the information is important, you should also list it in your resume.

You can source ideas for cover letters by completing an Internet search for "sample cover page letters for job applications".

If a phone number is listed for a contact person for the position, wherever possible always speak to them. They should be able to give you a little more information about the position over the phone. For example, the size of the team, if the position is new, if someone is acting in the position or if someone has left it, the organisation's culture, the organisation's location and even more information about the manager. You can also ask what the most important requirements for the role are. Any additional information will help you. If you've taken the time to call you may end up with information that others don't have.

When applying for roles listed on job boards, one of the most important things is to make sure you're not applying for the same role with several recruiters or even the recruiter and the organisation itself.

Organisations may advertise themselves, but they will also ask one or two recruiters to look for suitable candidates on their behalf. So it's likely that you'll see an advertisement listed by more than one recruiter for the same position.

It can be a challenge to know if the role is the same one, as each recruiter and the organisation itself can word the job criteria in the advertisement differently. You'll need to check this out and only apply for the role through one source.

It's disappointing, but sometimes you may not even get an acknowledgement from a recruiter or recruitment agency that your application has safely arrived. You can request a "Read Receipt" or "Delivered Receipt" on the email you send, which will let you know that it has been received. If you don't receive an acknowledgement, you can call to check.

Ideally you should hear back from an organisation within five to seven working days to indicate if they're still interested in proceeding through the process or if you've not been successful.

"Whatever you hold in your mind on a consistent basis is exactly what you will experience in your life."
Tony Robbins

CHAPTER SIX

PROFESSIONAL DIGITAL FOOTPRINT

DIGITAL FOOTPRINT: WHAT DOES YOURS SAY ABOUT YOU?

What's a digital footprint? For recruitment purposes your digital footprint is any data, information, comments, pictures and videos referencing you that can be found online, including through an Internet search, or on Facebook or LinkedIn.

Social media is a great way to stay connected to friends and family. If your settings enable the public to see your social media pages, then potential employers and recruitment consultants will have access. Everything you post online forms part of your digital footprint. It enables people to get a glimpse of who you are.

Once your information is "out there" it's almost impossible to delete it. Everything you post can be copied and shared with others. Even if you set your settings to private, this doesn't stop those you know from sharing information on you with people outside your intimate, trusted circle. In other words, you don't have control over what happens to this information.

From my research, I would suggest that approximately 75 percent of hiring managers and recruiters check a candidate's online identity before bringing them in for an interview, in fact, before even talking to them.

Managing your digital footprint is therefore now an important part of your job application process. Whether you intended it to be or not, your digital footprint is your personal brand. What does yours say about you? Are you being rejected because of your social media identity?

Employers want to see how you present yourself, how you conduct yourself, whether you're a strong cultural fit with their organisation and what your communications skills are like. In other words, they want to see what type of person you are.

So you need to be aware that an organisation may decide that you have a strong resume and want to bring you in for an interview. This could change once they check your digital footprint on social media. Your Facebook page may show you bad-mouthing a previous or current employer, for example, or out partying and drinking during the week, or taking illegal drugs. A potential employer may decide that some of these types of images, or even the words you post, are in poor taste. You might find that all of a sudden you're no longer in the running.

You may say this isn't fair, because the information is meant to be private. But if you're putting it out there, it's open for others to see.

WHAT CAUSES POTENTIAL EMPLOYERS TO REJECT YOUR APPLICATION?

The negative

So what do employers find on social media that could prompt them to eliminate a candidate from consideration? The most common reasons relate to when a candidate has:

- posted provocative or inappropriate photographs or information

- posted information about them drinking or using drugs

- bad-mouthed a previous company or fellow employees

- poor communication skills

- made discriminatory comments related to race, gender or religion

- lied about qualifications and experience or background

- shared confidential information from previous employers

- been linked to criminal behaviour

- adopted an unprofessional screen name

- lied about an absence from work (such as with a "sickie")

- displayed aggressive inappropriate behaviour

- exhibited morals not in line with the organisation's values or culture

- demonstrated that they are a high-risk recruit.

WHAT CAUSES POTENTIAL EMPLOYERS TO MORE LIKELY HIRE YOU?

The positive

Employers who research candidates on social networking sites say they've found content that made them more likely to hire a candidate.

The most common reasons relate to when a candidate:

- presented a good feel for their personality that could be a good fit for a company and its culture

- posts background information on themselves that are supported by professional qualifications that suit the job

- was involved in the community in a positive way, such as through volunteering or helping others

- conveys a professional image on their digital footprint

- appears well rounded with a wide range of interests

- demonstrates great communication skills

- demonstrates creativity

- includes awards and accolades received

- has posted great references from others

- has interacted with the company's social media accounts

- had a large amount of followers or subscribers.

IS YOUR ONLINE BRAND HELPING YOU GET A JOB?

Search for yourself on the Internet. Type your name into the Internet search bar and see what comes up. This is what a potential employer or recruiter will do. You'll see what they see. If you have a Facebook or LinkedIn account, for example, your name will come up. If a potential employer clicked into your Facebook account today, would they see something that would harm your chances or enhance your chances of getting a job with them?

CLEAN UP YOUR FOOTPRINT

Once you've checked out your digital footprint, decide if you should work on improving it and make the changes yourself. If it's way too bad and needs serious work you can find useful tips by doing an Internet search for "clean up digital footprint". This will get you started. You can also pay some companies to clean up your footprint for you.

CREATE A LINKEDIN PROFILE

If you don't have a LinkedIn account, I strongly suggest you create one. LinkedIn is designed as a professional forum where you can highlight your strengths and capabilities. **LinkedIn is free**. It's an extension of your resume and a way of backing up what you've said in your resume. Having a professional LinkedIn page also adds additional credibility.

Make sure the photo you use is a professional one, following the principles discussed in Chapter 1.

Ask previous colleagues, managers or clients if they'll write a short recommendation for you. This will immediately add to your credibility. It will also help you stand out from other candidates who may not have a presence on LinkedIn.

Employers and recruiters now also search on LinkedIn to find potential candidates. In your profile you can therefore add that you're currently looking for the next role in your career. This may also motivate recruiters and organisations to contact you for a potential new role.

If other candidates have a professional LinkedIn profile and the employer can learn a little more about them, this could sway the employer and be an advantage. Be aware that your current employer can also see you're looking for your next role.

APPROPRIATE EMAIL ADDRESS AND PHONE MESSAGE

It's important to have an appropriate email address. Some prospective employers have not considered an application due to an inappropriate email address. Make sure the email address you're using on your resume is professional.

When looking for work also create a new voice message on your mobile phone that's welcoming, short and professional. For example, you could say, "Hi. You've contacted Kate. Please leave a message and number so I can call you back. Thank you."

CHECK OUT YOUR POTENTIAL NEW BOSS AND COMPANY

Use social media to see what people are saying about the new boss and/or company you want to work for. See if the company has a LinkedIn profile or Facebook page. Does your prospective boss have a social media profile you can look at to gain a better understanding of them before interview? Use this information to your advantage.

"The greatest leader is not necessarily the one who does the greatest things. He is the one that gets the people to do the greatest things."
Ronald Reagan

CHAPTER SEVEN

TRACKING POSITIONS AND STATUS

KEEPING ON TOP OF THINGS

Once you start applying for a number of roles, it can be difficult to track where you're up to in the process with each position. The last thing you want is for a potential employer to call and you sound confused about what role they're talking about. It can damage your chance of securing an interview. To help, I've included a link to a free Job Tracker Form at the end of this section.

Keeping your Job Tracker Form handy and regularly referring to it to keep yourself up-to-date will enable you to be professional in your responses.

Along with your Job Tracker Form you should keep copies of all the job descriptions you've applied for. Keeping all information in the same spot with easy access will work to your advantage.

The Job Tracker Form enables you to quickly see where you're up to with each role, who you applied to for the position and whether it was direct or through a recruiter. This way when an employer calls, you'll be able to quickly refer to the information on the form and know where you are in the process.

With the form you can also close roles, so you know that no further action is required. You can see what positions you are and aren't getting interviews for. With this information you could target efforts more effectively.

The form also enables you to capture any feedback given, so you can refer back to it and improve the next time.

The form also enables you to add appropriate dates of when to follow up on an application if you haven't heard back.

The Job Tracker Form will also help you apply for a specific role with only one recruiter or the organisation direct. If it looks similar to another role you've already applied for, simply ask who the position is with through a recruiter. Recruiters are obliged to inform you who the end organisation is.

Visit this link to download the FREE Job Tracker Form.

http://www.f2frecruitment.com.au/resources/application-tracker/

"When you make a choice you change the future."
Deepak Chopra

CHAPTER EIGHT

STATE OF MIND AND COMBATING NERVES

NERVES – A THREAT TO YOUR SUCCESS

Have you ever come out of an interview and said to yourself: "What was I thinking? I knew the answers to those questions but just couldn't get them out. My mind either went blank or I babbled on and on. I didn't show them who I really was and how I'm perfect for this position. I didn't answer the questions properly so they won't understand my full capability." This is usually caused by being extremely nervous. Even well-seasoned performers can still have a case of the nerves, they simply learn how to control them.

Nerves can cause physical changes to the level of chemicals in our bodies. This is due to our automatic primitive response to "flight or fight" when we perceive an eminent threat. These days this response isn't required for fighting off a wild animal, but it pops up in situations like public speaking or attending an interview.

Nerves can be caused by:

- being out of your comfort zone

- fear of failure or rejection

- rehashing previous bad experiences when being interviewed

- fear of not being in control and not knowing what will happen

- believing you have a lot at stake riding on the interview, which adds to the pressure

- fear of speaking in front of people, even an interview panel of three or four people

- not being prepared and not thinking about what questions may be asked in advance.

What happens when you're nervous?

You may recall a time when you were nervous previously, either at another interview, when giving a speech or when completing an exam. You may recall that some of the symptoms you experienced were:

- sweaty palms (one of the most common)

- shortness of breath or shallow breathing

- trembling voice

- accelerated heartbeat or pulse

- sick feeling in the stomach, commonly referred to as butterflies

- feeling scared, anxious, panicky

- your brain going blank and being lost for words

- self-doubt and negative internal self-talk

- shaking hands and feeling weak at the knees

- wanting to back out or cancel with an excuse or wanting to hide in a corner where no-one can find you.

These are all common symptoms and most people experience several when nervous. Some people can keep their nerves controlled and to a minimum which enables them to perform at their best during interview.

Allowing your nerves to get the better of you can damage your performance at interview and your chances of securing a new position.

HOW TO MINIMISE NERVES

In this section, I provide some strategies and information to help you minimise nerves. They take practice. If you don't practice, they'll be of little or no benefit. What I want you to do is to become a "shadow boxer".

Shadow boxing practice. Shadow boxing is when a boxer or fighter moves around by themselves throwing punches at the air. It's a popular exercise for honing their fighting techniques, conditioning their muscles and mentally preparing themselves before a fight.

Just like an athlete you need to practice and train for your interview. Become an interview warrior. Ask yourself, based on the job description, what sort of questions might you might have to answer. Think about your response and then say it out loud to yourself.

This is preparing your mind/brain (working that muscle) to practice responding to questions, in the same way as a shadow boxer practices. Rehearsing the interview will give you an edge. In your bonus Chapter 9, "Interview Tips", I've included the top seven questions employers ask and how best to answer them.

Rehearse your interview. Visualise yourself in front of the interview panel and rehearse out loud. If possible, do this in front of some friends or family and ask for honest feedback about your verbal and non-verbal communication styles. Alternatively, video yourself, replay it and critique yourself. If you video yourself, watch the video at least five times before you start to critique yourself. This is to get you used to seeing yourself on video. Most of us don't like seeing ourselves on video. Once you're used to it you can concentrate on your wording and body language rather than on your appearance. Highlight three to five things you can improve on and practice these.

Body language. Our body language can influence how confident we feel. Being confident can reduce our nerves. I've provided a link to a video of Amy Cuddy's talk on body language. If you're going to an interview, I suggest you take time to watch it. Amy covers an anti-nervousness technique called "Power Posing", which involves posing like a super hero for two minutes. You can be "Wonder

Women" or "Superman" or any other power posing super hero. I know it sounds a bit "out there", but research from Harvard University has shown a dramatic 25 percent reduction in the stress hormones produced in your body and 20 percent improvement in confidence from power posing, which can improve your performance at interview. So, watch what Amy has to say. You've got nothing to lose and everything to gain. More than 6.6 million people to date have thought her video worth watching.

http://www.f2frecruitment.com.au/latest-news/the-power-of-body-language/

Please note: If this link has been taken down when you try to access it, simply do an Internet search for "Amy Cuddy body language" and you should find it easily.

Positive self-talk. How we talk to ourselves can make a dramatic impact on how we perform in an interview. Humans are renowned for constantly putting ourselves down with negative self-talk. We're extremely good at negative self-talk and, as individuals, we do a better job of running ourselves down than anyone else on the planet. Let's replace negative thoughts with positive thoughts.

Think about this, for example. How would you talk to or coach a good friend, partner, child or sibling who was going for an interview? Wouldn't you help them by highlighting their strengths and reminding them of all the relevant experience they have that suits the role? Wouldn't you try to boost their confidence and be positive? Wouldn't you ask questions the interviewers might ask and get them to practice responding? Yes you would. So be that good friend and coach yourself.

Convert negative to positive self-talk

Negative self-talk	Positive self-talk replacement
I'm so hopeless at interviews. I fall to pieces and my nerves get the better of me. I just go blank.	This time I'm prepared and have practiced. I've done my research and am confident I can perform well. I know my stuff. Breathe …
What was I thinking? I'm not right for this role.	They saw enough in my resume to bring me in for an interview. They're too busy to waste their time on people who they aren't

	seriously interested in. Come on, I can do this. I'm an interview warrior!
What if they just focus on all the things I'm not strong on?	They've brought me in for interview and will be aware of these areas. They still want to see me. This is my chance. If they do bring up weaknesses, I can acknowledge each one and tell panel members how I'm correcting them.
Here we go again. Another interview where I'm going to feel like a failure and look stupid. Why do I keep putting myself through this?	This is a great opportunity. The more interviews I go to the better I get and the better chance I have of getting the next job. I learn something new from each interview. This time I've learned so many new things and am better prepared than ever. I'm going to ace this one.
I always feel like interviewers ask trick questions because they	They want me to be great, to succeed, otherwise they

want to trip me up. I never know how to answer them.

wouldn't have brought me in for an interview.

This is my opportunity to confirm that they were right to bring me in. If I don't understand a question, all I need to say, is "I don't understand the question. Could you please rephrase it?" There's nothing wrong with that. It's so much better than babbling on or heading down the wrong path. It also shows that I'm full of confidence and not afraid to ask.

They aren't trying to trick me. They want to see how I handle myself with a difficult question.

Anyway, I've got this. I know my stuff because I do it all the time. I'm good at this. I'm prepared this time.

Be prepared. The better prepared you are and the more you know what questions to expect, the more likely you'll be to recall your answers even if you're feeling nervous or stressed.

Do your research on the company and check out their website. Conduct an Internet search to see if you can find additional information that could be useful. Make sure you know how long it will take to get to your interview and where you can park if taking your car. Arrive early enough to pay for parking and give yourself enough time to sit at a coffee shop nearby. Use this time to calm yourself down. This also reduces stress as you won't be worrying about being on time or about traffic delays.

Visualise. Another technique you can use to calm your nerves is to visualise yourself going to interview feeling confident, doing a great job answering the questions and coming out feeling great. Visualise how great you'll feel about your performance, whatever the outcome.

Breathing. Before you go into interview calm yourself with slow, deep breaths. Stand tall and sit with a straight back. Don't hunch over. Breathe in through your nose counting to four and breath out through your nose counting to four. If you're breathing deeply you'll notice your shoulders rise and fall. When we're nervous we shallow breathe and find ourselves out of breath when trying to answers questions. Our voice trembles and you may feel like you're shaking. During interview, make a conscious effort to keep your breathing a little slower than normal.

Interviewer expectations. The interviewer or members of an interview panel will expect that you'll be nervous. They'll allow for this. A good interviewer will ask you ice breaker questions first, to give you a chance to settle into the interview. If they don't, remember to breathe.

Interviewers honestly expect to see nerves at the outset. Allow yourself time to settle into the interview so you perform to the best of your ability as it continues. Sometimes panel members are also nervous, as they want to do a good job and the experience can be new to them.

Don't try to read what interviewers might be thinking. You can misinterpret a serious face, for example, as an indicator that you're not doing well, when in fact the interviewer is just really concentrating on doing a good job.

"The measure of intelligence is the ability
to change."
Albert Einstein

BONUS CHAPTER NINE

INTERVIEW TIPS

BE PREPARED

Preparation. Being prepared is the key to a successful interview. Chapter 8, "State Of Mind and Combating Nerves", covers how to tackle your nerves, remain calm, prepare and practice so you're ready to be an interview warrior. Please read Chapter 8 well before going to an interview because you'll need some time to prepare appropriately.

Make sure you take a hard copy (printed) of your resume to interview, in case you're asked to refer to it.

Company website. Always check out the company's website before you go to your interview. Even if you looked at the website when completing your application, look at it again to refresh your memory. There might also be new information posted that could be helpful. From the website you might also be able to prepare a question to ask the interviewer or interview panel. It will show them that you're serious enough to have done your research.

I'm constantly astounded at how many people don't take the time to refer to an organisation's website when preparing an application for a job or a job interview. The website not only tells you in detail what the company does, it usually gives you an insight into its culture and values. It provides you with a feel for the company; who they are.

A lot of companies are now including their staff on their website. This will give you an idea of the people you'll be working with and your new manager's background. They might also list some common interests.

Interview panel. Make sure you know how many people will be on the interview panel. There's nothing worse than thinking one or two people might be interviewing you and then arriving and seeing four faces staring at you. Also ask for the names of those on the panel and what position they hold. This can help you understand the context of their questions a little more. Your recruiter or contact for the position will be able to provide you with this information.

See if the members of the panel are listed on the company's website. Check out if they have a LinkedIn profile or Facebook page for additional background information.

BEFORE THE INTERVIEW

Make sure you've looked up the address of the location of the interview the *day before* the interview. Know where you're going and allow plenty of time for traffic congestion. If you're driving make sure you know where to park. Make sure you have a couple of options in case one car park is full. Be at reception five minutes before your interview time.

Ideally arrive 25 to 30 minutes early and sit at a coffee shop nearby. This will alleviate some stress worrying about getting to the interview on time. Sit, relax and breathe, as outlined in Chapter 8.

Close your eyes and visualise greeting the panel, sitting in your chair looking at them and responding calmly and with confidence to their questions. You've got this. You've completed all your preparations for this opportunity. Now the most important thing is to stay calm.

Normally at the end of an interview you'll be asked if you have any questions. I strongly suggest that you have one or two questions ready to ask the interviewer or panel members. This does two things. First it shows that you're really interested in the job and have done your homework. Second it changes the dynamic and can lead to a more open discussion rather than straight questions and answers. Several examples of the type of questions you could ask are listed here:

- What would be the expectations of me in a month, three months and 12 months?

- How would you describe the company culture?

- What's the biggest challenge facing the company?

- What has been the company's biggest success to date?

- What's your favourite part about working here?

A great question to use would be something you've discovered from the company website. You could say, for example: "I noticed on your website that the company is looking at expanding overseas. What countries are you going to target and why?" Another example: "I noticed on your website that you won an award. That's exciting. Could you tell me a little more about that?"

The company may have been in the media recently. If that's the case then a sample question could be: "I recently read that you're opening another branch in Canberra. What do you see will be the main challenges?"

PRESENTATION

Dress for success. It's always better to overdress for an interview than to be dressed too casually. Different positions require different levels of dress. For example, a corporate position requires a business suit, a blue collar job requires a smart shirt and smart casual pant or skirt. Whichever it is, leave the oversized hand bag or large man pouch behind. Keep your look clean and de-cluttered. It's ideal to simply take in a folder that has a notepad with a pen inside. The more you have to carry the more awkward you look when picking everything up and trying to get yourself organised to shake someone's hand.

Well-groomed. Make sure your shoes are polished and are not old and scruffy. If you're wearing nail polish make sure it's not chipped. Your clothes should be clean, ironed and not crumpled. Ideally, you should have an interview outfit that's in your wardrobe ready to go at the drop of a hat. If a company rang and asked you to come in for interview that afternoon or the next morning, are ready to go? If you are, this could be an advantage.

It doesn't matter what type of role you're going for, you should always be well-groomed. It's the simple things, like clean and tidy hair, that makes a difference. I can tell you that some of my clients are turned off right from the beginning of an interview when presented with someone who couldn't bother to present well. They asked themselves whether the candidates would present like this at work every day.

Stay away from alcohol and garlic the night before an interview. Some people find the smell of garlic off-putting. If you come to the interview reeking of alcohol the interviewer could assume that you're a heavy drinker and that alcohol could affect your work.

Go easy on the perfume and cologne. You don't want to overpower the interviewer and, besides, some people are allergic to these substances. Also be mindful that when you're nervous you tend to perspire more. If you have a tendency to perspire a lot, you may want to invest in an extra strength antiperspirant from a chemist.

GREETING AND HANDSHAKE

Stand, don't sit. When you arrive for interview, someone will usually greet you, let you know the panel won't be long and invite you to sit down. Some chairs can be difficult to get in and out of. When an interviewer greets you they usually offer their hand to shake before you've had the chance to stand up and collect your things. A handshake is extremely important. Sitting doesn't enable you to have control over your best handshake. I suggest standing while waiting. This way when the interviewer approaches you, you're not hunched in a chair but rather are ready to shake their hand immediately.

Hold your folder or other items with your left arm, leaving your right hand free to do a handshake without moving things awkwardly around.

The handshake. Your handshake should be firm (but not too firm). Pulse up and down two to three times and then release. While you're shaking someone's hand remember to smile and repeat their name. For example, "Good to meet you Kate." This builds rapport straight away and hopefully will help you remember their name when saying goodbye. This is especially important when there's a number of people on the interview panel.

Sweaty palms. Many people suffer from sweaty palms when they're nervous. A sweaty palm isn't your best first impression. One tip for this is to keep a hanky in the right pocket of your pants, skirt or dress. As you see or hear people coming, pop your hand in your pocket around the hanky and then bring it out to shake hands. It should be a lot drier. If you don't have a pocket simply hold the hanky in your right hand and then place it back into your folder as people are approaching.

Another tip is to wash your hands, dry them thoroughly and apply an antiperspirant onto your palms. Don't use hand lotion.

Here's a link to a video that highlights what not to do when shaking hands:

http://www.f2frecruitment.com.au/latest-news/the-top-10-bad-business-handshakes/

THE INTERVIEW

Interview warrior. To be an interview warrior, you have to remember to control your breathing. This will make such a difference to how you sound and how you think.

When you're an interview warrior and have prepared for your interview you'll be the best you can be. Stay calm and smile at your interviewers. Maintain eye contact with everyone on the panel (don't leave anyone out). If one panel member is constantly taking notes, make sure you catch them when they look up and then smile directly at them.

Sometimes panel members are so busy taking notes, they forget to give you positive reinforcement with a smile and eye contact. Don't let this put you off. It doesn't mean they're not interested or that you're not doing well. It's more likely that a panel member hasn't had appropriate training on how to conduct interviews. Stay positive and keep that smile on your face.

If you're asked a question and don't understand it, that's OK. It's fine to say you're not sure you understand the question and ask if the panel members can rephrase it for you. This is a much better option than going off on a tangent and answering it incorrectly. It also shows that you're confident.

Don't rush into an answer. Give yourself a couple of seconds to think before responding. And breathe.

Positive last impression. Genuinely thank panel members for providing you with the opportunity to present yourself. Shake everyone's hand to say goodbye, use names if you remember them and smile. Vary your goodbyes. To one person, you may say, "Thank you Kate." To another you may say, "It was a pleasure meeting you, Alex." Leaving the room on a professional and controlled note is as important as starting on a professional and controlled note.

After the interview send a brief email thanking interviewers for their time and consideration. This can leave them with another positive experience of you. Reiterating your interest in the role could tip them in your direction. Don't go over the top, however. You're not reselling yourself here, you're just briefly thanking the members of the interview panel – nothing more.

Confidence is key. When responding to questions, be confident, speak clearly and make sure you're loud enough that everyone can hear what you're saying. Don't waste your answers.

Remember, if you're nervous you'll have a tendency to speak too quickly. Be aware of this and slow yourself down. This also gives you more time to think about what to say next.

If you catch yourself babbling, stop immediately and say, "Sorry I'm nervous and went off on a tangent. What I really want to say is ..." Panel members will appreciate your self-awareness and ability to pull yourself back on track.

Don't be negative about employers. When responding to questions never be negative about a previous employer or company. There's always a way to answer a question without being negative.

Example

Question: Why are you leaving your current position?

Negative response: My boss is a micro-manager and never lets me do anything. They have no idea how to manage people and develop them. It's an awful environment and they have no idea what they're doing.

Better response: I'm looking for a new challenge where I can learn and develop my skills to another level. I'm excited and ready for the next phase in my career.

WHAT NOT TO DO DURING INTERVIEW

- Never turn up late. If you have no choice, call ahead and let them know.

- Never go into an interview unprepared. Do your research.

- Don't turn up inappropriately dressed, wearing revealing or overly casual clothing.

- Don't underdress. Always go up a couple of levels.

- Don't overload on the aftershave or perfume, since this can be overbearing and cause headaches.

- Don't, on the other hand, smell with body odour, which is off-putting.

- Don't turn up smelling like cigarettes, alcohol or garlic.

- Don't bad mouth previous employers or tell horror stories about companies or staff.

- Never answer a call on your phone. Turn it off. Don't even leave it on vibrate.

- Never chew gum during an interview.

- Don't slouch. Good posture makes you look more professional and alert.

- Don't fidget with your phone or a pen. Stay focused.

- Don't start answers with "um" or "ah".

- Don't ramble on and on when answering a question. Stay on point.

- Don't avoid eye contact. This can be misinterpreted as lack of confidence or interest or weak interpersonal skills.

- Never give a weak handshake or a handshake that's too hard.

- Never interrupt someone who is talking.

- Never swear or use slang during an interview, even if the interviewer is using it.

- Don't become too familiar with people.

- Don't discuss money, unless the interviewers bring it up (if working with a recruiter, refer them back to the recruiter for salary negotiations).

- Never lie.

- Don't ask for flexible hours before you even start.

- Don't be arrogant.

- Never just sit down. Wait to be offered a seat. This shows a high level of etiquette and manners.

TOP SEVEN INTERVIEW QUESTIONS AND RESPONSES

Anytime you're responding to interview questions, you should consider how your experience relates back to the company interviewing you. By pre-preparing for some of the most common questions, you'll be able to provide relevant and concise responses. You'll also be more confident since you'll have thought about examples to use that show your experience or expertise.

By working through questions and preparing in advance you won't get flustered trying to think of the perfect example on the spot at interview. Rehearse your responses out loud or to a friend. You don't need to remember your response word for word, just the main points of what you want to cover. If your answer is too rehearsed it won't sound authentic.

COMMONLY ASKED QUESTIONS

1. Tell me a little about yourself?

This can be the first question you're asked at interview. It's regularly used as an ice breaker. The interviewers aren't asking for your life story. Your response should be no more than two minutes. This doesn't sound like a long time but you can fit a lot of words and information into two minutes. Time your rehearsals.

With your answer, you can provide some personal information about your interests, such as sports, reading or volunteering. You could then go into the personal attributes you think are aligned with the position or the company. These are the soft skills that aren't always evident in your resume. Examples are your work ethic or core values if they align with the company's (check for them on the company website). Finish your response with your top two key strengths and skills that are perfect for the role and will benefit your potential new employer. Don't be shy.

If you do this well and with confidence, you'll have started extremely well and set the tone for the interview.

2. What has attracted you to apply for a position with us?

This is your opportunity to show how enthusiastic you are about the position. Interviewers want to see that you're genuine in wanting to work for them and not just applying for any job. You can start by saying that when you saw the advertisement you were excited as you thought your key skills and strengths and background are a great match. Make sure you provide examples of how this is so. Describe that when you researched the company you saw how your core values are aligned, how you like their approach, and/or how passionate you are about the industry they're in or their community focus. Talk about whatever it was that made you want to work for this organisation. The more authentic you are with your answers the better you'll come across.

This is a great opportunity to talk about some of your personality traits that would help in this position. It could be your drive and determination, your proactive approach, your lateral thinking, your enthusiasm in mentoring others, or any other relevant soft skills.

3. What would you describe as your key strengths? (This is one of the most common questions.)
This is where you can highlight the key strengths you hold that are relevant to the role. Make sure you have two to three examples ready that demonstrate where you've shone in the past and how this will help in the position.

Your strengths could be the ability to stay calm under pressure, that you're a quick learner, are great with procedures and processes that save time, have drive and determination, a positive "can-do" attitude, an ability to research, problem solving skills and an ability to think laterally. Whatever your strengths are, make sure you back them with examples of where you've used them in the past and the positive outcomes achieved as a result.

4. What are your weaknesses? (This is one of the most common questions.)

We all have weaknesses and interviewers know that. They're just seeing that you're aware of what yours might be. They're also interested in how you handle yourself when you're being asked for a negative about yourself.

This is a great example of how being prepared enables you to stand out from others. Always select a weakness that's not key to the role. Interviewers want to see that you're capable of understanding your weaknesses and want to improve and develop. Here's a clever way of responding using something that may not necessarily be a true weakness.

Perceived weakness. "People say I'm at times over enthusiastic and they feel pressured to keep up with me."

Correction and improvement. "I'm now aware that not everyone operates at the same levels and I'm more conscious of improving my awareness of how others prefer to work and take more of a collaborative approach."

Showing a willingness to develop yourself and being able to display self-awareness turns your response into a positive.

5. What have been your greatest career achievements to date?

Think of one or two accomplishments you had in your past positions and provide examples of achievements that relate to the position you're interviewing for. Specify what it was, what your actions were, what you did to achieve a positive result and what that result was. If you reduced costs by, say, 20 percent, or improved a process, saving time, it would be advantageous to mention the exact savings or reduction in time. Don't, for example, say you implemented energy efficiency steps in the office to reduce emissions. Say you implemented energy efficiency steps in the office and reduced emissions by 30 percent. Can you see how that's much stronger?

Frame this type of information so it emphasises your credibility as a high-achiever, an attribute any company would want.

6. Do you have any questions? (This question is usually asked at every interview.)

Note: This information is also listed under "Before the Interview" in this chapter. I'm repeating it here as it's usually asked in every interview situation.

Usually at the end of an interview you'll be asked if you have any questions. I strongly suggest that you have one to two questions ready. This does two things. First it shows that you're really interested and have done your homework. Second, it changes the dynamic by asking the panel questions and can lead to a more open discussion rather than straight questions and answers. Several examples of the types of question you might ask are listed here:

- What would be the expectations of myself in a month, three months and 12 months?

- How would you describe the company culture?

- What's the biggest challenge facing the company?

- What has been the company's biggest success to date?

- What's your favourite part about working here?

A great question would be something you discovered from the company website. You could say, for example: "I noticed on your website that the company is looking at expanding overseas. What countries are you going to target and why?" Another: "I noticed on your website you won an award, could you tell me a little more about that?"

The company may have been in the media recently. A sample question could be: "I recently read that you're opening another branch in Canberra. What do you see will be the main challenges?"

7. Why are you leaving your current role? Why have you left your previous position?

This question can be tricky. Make sure you give a short and clear answer. There's no need to go into too much detail. Remember to stay positive no matter what your situation is. Be as honest as possible. You may have enjoyed your time with your present employer but have found since their recent restructure or buy-out that the organisation is no longer the same. It could be because you've been there for some time, feel you've done as much as you can in your current role and are now looking for more challenging work and/or more responsibility. You could have completed a degree or additional training and are now looking to use your newly gained knowledge.

If you're leaving because of your manager or a bad working environment, a response could be that you feel you've outgrown the current environment and are looking for something inspiring and fresh.

Other questions to consider:

- Which one of your previous positions have you enjoyed the most/the least?

- What are your long-term goals?

- What do you know about our company?

- What are your salary expectations?

- How do you deal with stressful situations and working under pressure?

- What motivates you?

- What are you passionate about?

- What's your management style?

- What management style would you work best with?

- Why should we hire you?

- Are you being interviewed for other roles?

- Give me an example of when you haven't got along with co-workers or bosses. How did you handle it?

- What are you looking for in a company?

- How do you measure your own performance?

HANDLING UNUSUAL INTERVIEW QUESTIONS

- Are you a self-starter? Give me examples to demonstrate this.

- What can you bring to the table that benefits our company?

Some interviewers will throw in a random question. It will usually be one you haven't prepared for. There will be no right or wrong response. The question is designed to see how you think on your feet. To see if it throws you off. They might be looking at your approach to solving a problem, or if you can think laterally or simply how you handle the question. They might also be looking for creativity or if you have a sense of humour. Don't overthink. Have some fun with the answer.

Again, before answering the question, pause, breathe and then respond. Give your answer and the rationale for your response.

A couple of sample questions

- If you were an animal, what would you be?

- What animal best describes you?

- If you were a colour, what colour would you be?

Here are common descriptions of what people associate with a particular animal

- fox – clever, with a bit of slyness

- tiger – intelligent, street smart

- lion – the boss, fighter, a warrior, above all others, asserts authority

- elephant – leader, unstoppable, dependable, never forgets anything

- monkey – intelligent, nimble and a little cheeky

- ant – hard worker, never stops

- dolphin – highly intelligent and loveable

- butterfly – always in one stage or another of development

- chameleon – blends in, not one to stand out

- owl – wise, good at seeing the big picture

- dove – peacemaker.

These guys don't get such a good rap

- snake – sneaky and dishonest

- sloth – lazy

- shark – cold, ruthless, aggressive

Another question

If you were deserted on an island and could choose three things to take, what would they be and why?

You might answer, "a canopy, matches and water", which shows you're practical. You might answer 'my best friend, lots of books and resort clothing", which shows your creative, fun side.

WHAT'S A BEHAVIOURAL QUESTION AND HOW DO YOU ANSWER THEM?

Behavioural interview questions are becoming more and more part of the interview process. Whether the interview is with an employer or recruiter, employers are using these types of questions to get an idea of whether you have the skills required for the job. Behavioural questions test how you performed in the past, as this is most likely how you will perform in the future. It provides the employer with a view of your level of competency. Government departments now regularly use this form of interview questioning.

With these types of questions you usually start with a story of what the problem is. You then move on to how you went about finding a solution, how you implemented that solution and the resulting outcome and benefits. However, your response needs to be no more than two minutes long. It's best to rehearse this so you don't get off track and babble on. Your story should highlight the skills you used to perform the role.

Format used to respond to behavioural questions

Employers usually expect that candidates will know and respond to these types of questions using the STAR format.

Situation. What was the challenge? The interviewer wants you to present a recent challenge and situation in which you found yourself.

Task. What did you have to achieve? The interviewer will be looking to see what you were trying to achieve from the situation.

Action. What did you do? The interviewer will be looking for information on what you did, why you did it and the alternatives you thought through.

Results. What were the outcomes of your actions? What did you achieve through your actions and did you meet your objectives? What did you learn from this experience and have you used this learning since?

How to respond to behavioural interviews

In the following example, the **STAR** method described earlier can be used.

Example

Situation – Role as Research Support Officer at the Department of ABC.

Task – Needed to ensure that managers were kept informed changes to of policies and procedures.

Action – Initiated monthly newsletter, which was emailed to each manager. Took responsibility for writing the main articles. This involved obtaining ideas and input from stakeholders to ensure that the articles reflected management needs (content and language).

Result – Feedback was consistently excellent. Received divisional achievement award for newsletter quality. Led to improved lines of communication between managers and Research Support Unit.

Once you've developed your framework response you can then transform it into a story. The following example takes approximately 45 seconds to tell. Your responses should never take more than two minutes. This is a great example of a concise and effective response.

Example

"As Research Support Officer at the Department of ABC, I needed to ensure that managers were kept informed of changing policies and procedures. To do this, I initiated a monthly newsletter, which was emailed to each manager. I took responsibility for writing the main articles in each publication. This involved obtaining ideas and input from stakeholders to ensure the articles reflected the needs of management, both in content and language. I consistently received excellent feedback on the newsletter from these internal clients and my own manager. I received a divisional achievement award for the quality of the newsletter from management. Importantly, this initiative resulted in improved lines of communication between managers and the Research Support Unit".

Behavioural responses will take some practice. To find out more about these you can do an Internet search on: "star format examples".

TEN OF THE MOST ASKED BEHAVIOURAL SCENARIOS

1. Describe a time when you faced a stressful situation and how you overcame the situation.

2. Describe a situation when you had to think on your feet to make an instant decision.

3. Give me an example of a time when you motivated others and how this led to a positive outcome.

4. Provide an example of a goal you set and how you reached it.

5. Describe a situation where you knew your boss was wrong and how you handled it.

6. Provide an example of when you had to go above and beyond your normal duties to get a job done.

7. Provide an example of a problem or conflict you had with a colleague or manager and how you resolved it.

8. Describe a time when you weren't performing at work and what you did about it.

9. Tell me about a time when you went overtime on a deadline.

10. Discuss a setback you have overcome in the last 12 months.

RESPONDING TO INAPPROPRIATE QUESTIONS

People conducting interviews should know the difference between acceptable questions and discriminatory questions. However, this isn't always the case. A lot of interviewers in the private sector have limited experience in interviewing people. Government interviewers are usually well trained in what is or is not acceptable. You as the interviewee should also know your rights and this will enable to you know when a question is inappropriate.

Any questions that reveal your age, race, national origin, gender, religion, marital status and sexual orientation are off limits.

Australian Government and state and territory government laws make discrimination based on certain protected categories illegal. This includes national origin, citizenship, age, marital status, disabilities, arrest and conviction record, military discharge status, race, gender and pregnancy status.

SOME INAPPROPRIATE QUESTIONS

- How old are you?

- What's your date of birth?

- Do you speak English at home?

- How many sick days did you take last year?

- Are you married?

- Who cares for the children while you're working?

- Are you gay?

- Where were you born?

- Do you have children?

- Are you planning a family?

- Are you pregnant?

- Do you have a disability?

- Do you have health problems?

More information can be found out about these laws on the Australian Human Rights Commission's website:

https://www.humanrights.gov.au/employers/good-practice-good-business-factsheets/quick-guide-australian-discrimination-laws

Responding to inappropriate questions

If you're asked an inappropriate question you have a couple of options:

- You can choose to answer the question if you want to, but you need to be aware that if you provide the information, it could be held against you.

- You can refuse to answer the question or ask the interviewer to clarify how it's relevant to the job. Obviously, you want to be as pleasant and professional as possible in the way you do this, remembering that some interviewers may not be aware they're asking an inappropriate question.

- For example: I'm not sure of the relevance of the question to this position or my ability to do the job. Perhaps you could explain why you think it's important and I'll try to answer in a way that's relevant to the job.

"There are no shortcuts to any place worth going."

Oprah Winfrey

ABOUT THE AUTHOR

Kate Prior, Managing Director

Kate was raised on the New South Wales coast at beautiful Milton-Ulladulla. At 17 years of age, she courageously moved to Canberra by herself, knowing not a soul. Although her home town is gorgeous, Kate knew that to forge the career she wanted she needed to move to a city.

Kate has more than 23 years' experience in recruitment and is considered an expert in her field. She is regularly in the media commenting on recruitment topics and providing information and advice.

In 2005, Kate started her own recruitment company, called face2face Recruitment. In 2010, Kate led her company to win a national award for Australian Small Business Champion for Recruitment Services. In 2012, face2face Recruitment was runner up for the same award.

Kate has faced her own set of challenges throughout her career. She has been made redundant right before Christmas and lost a job she loved due to a company restructuring and listing on the stock exchange. Kate understands what losing a job feels like and the pressure people face in finding another position to cover the bills.

Every day Kate meets people trying to find work and her advice is always the same. That's why she wrote this book, to give everyone the chance to unravel some of the secrets to finding a great job.

Kate finds it amusing that there's an assumption that if you're looking for work, you should automatically be an expert at it. Wouldn't you already know how to create a perfect resume or prepare for an interview? Of course not. Like anything else we do, we get training. Well this book is your training.

"I know how hard it is for people finding work. All the pressure that's on them. I wanted to create a tool that would help them quickly and easily find a new role or move from a role they dislike," says Kate.

www.f2frecruitment.com.au

www.facebook.com/f2frecruitment

"You get in life what you have the courage to ask for."
Nancy D Solomon

ISBN: 978-0-9944771-1-8 (paperback)

"The adventure of life is to learn. The purpose of life is to grow. The nature of life is to change. The challenge of life is to overcome. The essence of life is to care. The opportunity of life is to serve. The secret of life is to dare. The spice of life is to befriend. The beauty of life is to give."
William Arthur Ward

www.ingramcontent.com/pod-product-compliance
Lightning Source LLC
Chambersburg PA
CBHW070731220326
41598CB00024BA/3392